One Heart,
One Breath,
One Soul,
One Me

Sharing Inspiration, Wisdom,
Guidance and Empowerment

with Gaye Piper

BALBOA
PRESS
A DIVISION OF HAY HOUSE

Also by Gaye Piper

MEDITATION CDs
What is Meditation?
Meditations of Moment
Clearing the Blockages and Challenges of Dis-ease in the Body
Meditation of Soul – Clearing, Cleansing,
Releasement and Energising
Receiving Your Angel Wings

Plus... a variety of live meditations channelled
at Gaye's weekly meditation group

CARD DECK
Your Spiritual and Energy Anatomy Q&A - 64 cards
(A fun way of learning and a powerful study companion)

All of the above may be ordered by visiting
www.gayepiper.com

Copyright © 2011 Gaye Piper

All rights reserved. No part of this book may be used or reproduced by any means, graphic, electronic, or mechanical, including photocopying, recording, taping or by any information storage retrieval system without the written permission of the publisher except in the case of brief quotations embodied in critical articles and reviews.

www.gayepiper.com
Email: angelonics@hotmail.com
Photography: Rodney Shrimpton, Australia

Balboa Press books may be ordered through booksellers or by contacting:

Balboa Press
A Division of Hay House
1663 Liberty Drive
Bloomington, IN 47403
www.balboapress.com
1-(877) 407-4847

Because of the dynamic nature of the Internet, any Web addresses or links contained in this book may have changed since publication and may no longer be valid. The views expressed in this work are solely those of the author and do not necessarily reflect the views of the publisher, and the publisher hereby disclaims any responsibility for them.

The author of this book does not dispense medical advice or prescribe the use of any technique as a form of treatment for physical, emotional, or medical problems without the advice of a physician, either directly or indirectly. The intent of the author is only to offer information of a general nature to help you in your quest for emotional and spiritual well-being. In the event you use any of the information in this book for yourself, which is your constitutional right, the author and the publisher assume no responsibility for your actions.

ISBN: 978-1-4525-0122-2 (sc)
ISBN: 978-1-4525-0124-6 (dj)
ISBN: 978-1-4525-0123-9 (e)

Library of Congress Control Number: 2010916291

Any people depicted in stock imagery provided by Thinkstock are models, and such images are being used for illustrative purposes only.
Certain stock imagery © Thinkstock.

Printed in the United States of America

Balboa Press rev. date: 1/14/2011

Everything starts with a Thought

Then an Idea

Followed by Creation

To my five beautiful children whom I love and adore so much and have great appreciation of; Todd, Crystal, Ryan, Allira and Brock, and for them just being the unique people they are – an important part of my Soul's journey - together with the partners they have chosen to share their lives with.

To my very precious granddaughter, Lily Grace and to the two new grandchildren waiting to join our family, Bump and Bean, who before they were born, I met with on the Soul plane and for all the future wisdom they bring to my life and those whom they share their lives with.

Preface

The Title of this book, One Heart, One Breath, One Soul, One Me, may seem that it is only about the author, but it is about the "essence" of the "One" of each and every one of ourselves, our own individualism and our own oneness with the Divine.

My journey thus far has taken me to the many recesses of my mind, body and spirit and unbeknowns to me, the writings in my Spiritual Journal was to play an intricate part of this book.

I have known for some time that one of my purposes was/is/will be to encourage empowerment of self and others but did not know the way in which this would actually be achieved.

I speculated that it would be, initially, through my own self or through my workshops, weekly meditation and discussion group, my unique meditation CDs, my spiritual cards on Q&A of the Spiritual and Energy Anatomy and all this is true but never in my wildest dreams considered that it would be this book... One Heart, One Breath, One Soul, One Me.

I was guided, and I truly do mean guided, to put together in this book an overflowing of wealth of Universal messages.

This book is a reflection of self, the truths that have empowered me through many challenging times and was uniquely guided to put my thoughts forward to allow YOU to empower yourself and know that you are a beacon of light.

We all have this and we all can do this. We just need the courage, the trust and the faith and step forward into the brilliance of the unknown of Universal Love and Energy and the complete oneness of ourselves.

I trust my words bring a deeper understanding to your life and know you are a most special person in this world and you are worth it and you do make a difference.

Heartfelt gratitude to all the amazing Teachers I have studied with thus far, whether in person or in spirit, in books, on CDs and DVDs, friends and family. Each and everyone have made a profound impact on my life and I am so grateful that we honoured our Soul agreements. Thank you.

How you receive inspiration and guidance can be in many different ways, so don't limit yourself in how your teachings come through... just be open to the positive messages and guidance that come your way and record it in a Spiritual Journal, for you never know when the things that you write become so much more than you think.

I so know this to be true.

Enjoy the truth that is of all of us, if we allow and live your dream.

In light, love and blessings - Gaye Piper
Orange, NSW, Australia

www.gayepiper.com

Acknowledgements

To my friends, Brianna Williams, Tania Chilby and Sue Pardey, your belief, encouragement and support is always Soul lifting and very appreciated.

To Kim Fraser (Shakti Durga), my first Mentor and teacher. Our years of journeying together are a most precious gift and my heart is full of gratitude and appreciation.

To my Crystal Master, Raym – journeying into the different realms that you have shown and taught me is such a gift of knowledge.

To the Harmonic Accord of Il Divo – the vibration and harmony of their voices, dances with, and opens my Soul even more, it is a complete resonance of the fine tuning of my Soul with their music. Find your music vibration to dance with.

To Dr Anthony and Mrs Chan - thank you for being the people you are.

To Rodney Shrimpton for the beautiful photos that you create and capture.

To the wisdom of my Soul and the allowance of my humanness to bring forth the Universal energy and inspiration that is abound.

And finally, to all that have touched my life in the many different ways both negative and positive – for they all have a place in the balance of all.

Namaste

Allow me to be a reason, a season or a lifetime in your life
and trust in whatever form this may take
and appreciate whichever it is.

and

Thank you to all who have been a reason, a season or a
lifetime on my journey, for each and every one of you have
made a profound difference in my life.

Namaste - Gaye Piper

A REASON...

      A SEASON...

            OR A LIFETIME

REASON

When someone is in your life for a REASON... It is usually to meet a need you have expressed. They have come to assist you through a difficulty, to provide you with guidance and support, to aid you physically, emotionally, or spiritually. They may seem like a godsend, and they are! They are there for the reason you need them to be.

Then, without any wrong doing on your part, or at an inconvenient time, this person will say or do something to bring the relationship to an end.

Sometimes they die. Sometimes they walk away. Sometimes they act up and force you to take a stand. What we must realize is that our need has been met, our desire fulfilled, their work is done.

The prayer you sent up has been answered. And now it is time to move on.

SEASON

Then people come into your life for a SEASON.

Because your turn has come to share, grow, or learn.

They bring you an experience of peace, or make you laugh.

They may teach you something you have never done.

They usually give you an unbelievable amount of joy.

Believe it! It is real!

But, only for a season.

LIFETIME

LIFETIME relationships teach you lifetime lessons; things you must build upon in order to have a solid emotional foundation.

Your job is to accept the lesson, love the person, and put what you have learned to use in all other relationships and areas of your life.

It is said that love is blind but friendship is clairvoyant.

THANK YOU for being a part of my life... whether it is for a reason...
        a season...
                or a lifetime

                                      Original Author Unknown

Within family there is strength

Outside family there is strength

Believe it is so

It is there

Draw from the strength of those who have the wisdom to share it

I share mine

To know Soul

is

Peace

To feel Soul

is

Pure Bliss

To hear Soul

is

the Universal Heart Beat

The Universal Heart Beat

is just

a whisper away

~

Listen

Dance like no one is watching

Sing like no one is listening

Love like you've never been hurt and

Live like it's heaven on earth

> by Mark Twain

Be brave

Take the bricks and wall
away from the truth
of who you are

Allow the light that is
you to shine through

You can do it

You are worth it

Take a chance on you

Allow the tears
from the Soul
to flow through your eyes
and honour yourself
in the process

Through adversity comes growth

Journey through it and have the trust and the faith in the gifts it can bring for even through the harshest of times, if you allow, the learning is there

~

just allow yourself the time to reach it

Live the life

you

were meant to live

Embrace realisations both
negative and positive

They both have a place
in your journey

Psychic is Greek for

"of the Soul"

Awaken to the Soul
and feel its love

Allow the peace to flow

Connection to Soul brings growth

Listening to Soul brings
much completeness

Know the wisdom of Soul
balances all out

Trust in <u>your</u> Soul

Close your eyes and find
Soul within you

Allow your concentrated awareness
to find the energy of your Soul

Allow your Soul's vibration
to talk with you

It takes 3-8 confluent sounds of the Harmonic Accord to completely open the 3rd eye

Ask yourself in full truthfulness

What do I really desire?

What makes me really happy?

The brilliance of who you
are is always there

Dwelling inside you

No matter what is going on

in your life,

the light is always there

When you can allow the light

~

It will grow more and more

~

It will grow brighter and brighter

~

Bringing out the sheer radiance
of who you are and when you can
feel or sense this, believe it is so

Trust in yourself

Allow you to become your own beacon

It starts with you...

Allow the true essence

of you

to keep coming forward

*Just believe
and intend
for all to be so…*

And so it shall be

When you allow the
relaxation process, feel the
swath of the energy flow
down,
down,
down
over the entirety of your body

And you are letting go

It is time to allow
all the beautiful things
you desire in your life
and allow your mind
to flood these into your body

Imagine and visualise
all
the positive and loving things
you desire in your life
and
breathe them into your
body
mind and
spirit

Allow yourself to go
beyond the confines of
who you are...
what you have...
and
what you desire in this life

Now is the time to
reach for the stars

Reach for your true destiny

And allow the inspiration of
you to speak with you

Now is the time to reach for your full potential

... allow this to be

Allow your mind to create
what you desire in your life

What you deserve in your life

What you choose to have in your life

See it

Feel it

Know it

And then from the mind, take it to
your heart centre and send it out from
your heart centre with all the love
of self and the Universal breath

Remember energy follows thought

Allow your thoughts to be wholesome
and
then allow and trust
in the magic that is you
and the Universe

Put a smile on your face

Mean it

Feel it

Allow it

This smile is just for you

Don't struggle

Allow the smile to be true

For as you smile at yourself, the energies around smile back at you

A smile says a thousand words

A smile brightens the heart

A smile lets you know you are special

A smile is a friend

A smile just for you

My smile is just for you

Know that you do make a difference

Remember to smile at yourself several times a day and say to yourself

I love you

I am special

And I am so worth it

Allow this smile to grow more and more in your heart centre and as you do, it is like a most precious, good and loving feeling overflowing and you are able to send this beautiful abundance of good and loving energy out to all and as this process happens, this precious energy flows all over you as well

Bathe in it

Allow gratitude to touch you

Allow your gratitude to touch others

Allow the humbleness of
gratitude to expand all that
is of you and your world

Do you know me?

Do you desire to know who I am?

I am THEY

The
Higher
Essence of
You

I am the God

I am the Angels

I am the Soul

I am... YOU

For this all dwells within

Age is no barrier
for the gifts
that is abundant and
ready to "pull in"
and
the lessons of life's riches

Honour yourself in the quiet moments of your mind

I invest in myself

Be the strength you deserve

I am who I am

A loving wholesome human being

To engage in life

I need to have

the faith in myself

I believe

I believe

I believe in me

One should never assume

that one can't do it

Give yourself the freedom

in all its entirety

You are free to be who you are

~

if you chose to be

Allow the heart to breathe

Creation is the inspiration within and without

Allow the dreaming time

to release and

bring you closer to your truth

Have the courage

to bring your potential

to the forefront and

be proactive

in an experience of journey

Be resplendent

in the midst of all

Close your eyes

Go to the beat of your heart

Allow it
Feel it
Be it

Let the beat of your heart
sound throughout your body.
Allow the vibration of your heart beat
to grow and grow within your mind.

Know that this heart beat, when
sent to all parts of your body has the
most powerful gift of all – LIFE

We are all the uniqueness of
the oneness of ourselves

~The Me~

~The I~

I am one

of the nicest people

you can have

in your life

Information is knowledge

Knowledge is empowering

Empowering is powerful

and

Powerful is YOU

Take the positive and allow
that to dwell within

The negative is always hiding
there, make it a friend.

For when you do,
a friend always wants the best
for you in a most positive way

and shine you will

TWO WOLVES

One evening an old Cherokee told his grandson about a battle that goes on inside all people.

He said, "My son, the battle is between two 'wolves' inside us all."

One is Evil. It is anger, envy, jealousy, sorrow, regret, greed, arrogance, self-pity, guilt, resentment, inferiority, lies, false pride, superiority, and ego.

The other is Good. It is joy, peace, love, hope, serenity, humility, kindness, benevolence, empathy, generosity, truth, compassion and faith.

The grandson thought about it for a minute and then asked his grandfather:

"Which wolf wins?"

The old Cherokee simply replied:

The one you feed

Original Author Unknown

Which one will you choose?

Simply – these are my truths

Glossary

Confluent
Flowing together
Blending into one
Merging
Running together

Me
The "essence" of the "One" of each and every one of ourselves, our own individualism and our own oneness with the Divine. Also known as the "I"

Resplendent
Having great beauty and splendour

Soul
    The soul has often been deemed integral or essential to consciousness and personality, and soul sometimes functions as a synonym for spirit, mind or self.
    Soul, for the Author, is the complete centre of knowingness of, and for, the journeys of life for each and everyone

THEY
THEY are a group consciousness from the non-physical dimension (that helps a lot).

Resources

The Akasha Holistic Directory – Orange and beyond
www.akashaholisticdirectory.com

Doreen Virtue, Ph.D.
www.AngelTherapy.com

Global Healing (Crystal Dreaming) - Raym
www.global-healing.com

Gregg Braden
www.greggbraden.com

Hay House
www.hayhouse.com

Holistic Page
www.holisticpage.com.au

The Journey - Brandon Bays
www.thejourney.com

Pranic Healing
www.pranichealing.com

Rainbow Lodge Spiritual Sanctuary Aust- Grahame McNaughton
www.rainbowspiritualsantuary.com.au

The Shanti Mission Harmony Centre – Shakti Durga
www.harmonycentrefoundation.org

Syngery I – Gaye Piper
www.gayepiper.com

References

Original Authors Unknown:
    A Reason, A Season, A Lifetime
    Two Wolves

Twain, Mark: *Poem untitled*

About the Author

Gaye Piper is the Founder and Director of Synergy I and

Founder, Administrator and Director of
The Akasha Holistic Directory – Orange and beyond

Gaye lives in Orange, New South Wales, Australia, is a Mum to 5 beautiful adult children, mother-in-law and Grammy and has endured many challenging times through her life. It is through these life teachings that she has been able to bring in the "tools" of her studies of positiveness, understanding, love and forgiveness that support her in an honoured way but not understating the journey through to the final outcome.

Gaye is dedicated to bringing the energies of the Spirit, the Soul and the Physical Dimensions into working together for a healthy, happy and peaceful lifestyle.

She is a Master Healer with a deep understating of the situations causing physical, mental, emotional and spiritual ill health and is passionate about "waking" people up to their own magnificence".

Through the amazing and talented Teachers that Gaye has studied with and who have touched her life, and the Soul Family she has connected with on this and the Spiritual plane, she is now able to bring these teachings to those who seek a similar path or just desire to improve their own lives.

This phase of Gaye's life is bringing forward a new dimension for her in writing books, creating unique mediation CDs and bringing forward the knowledge of our Spiritual and Energy anatomy in the way of Question and Answer cards, as well as her workshops, meditation groups and energy healings.

Gaye believes in "giving back" to her community in many different ways and embraces the life of this life time.

You can contact Gaye through her Website
www.gayepiper.com
or
www.akashaholisticdirectory.com

Your Thoughts

Your Thoughts

Your Thoughts

Your Thoughts

Your Thoughts

Your Thoughts

Your Thoughts

Your Thoughts

Your Thoughts

Your Thoughts

Your Thoughts

Your Thoughts

Your Thoughts

www.ingramcontent.com/pod-product-compliance
Lightning Source LLC
Chambersburg PA
CBHW020014050426
42450CB00005B/461